LOSING CASSIE, FINDING PEACE

One mother's journey from the loss of a child to belief in the "unproven proof" of life after death.

Kathy Matchinsky

With Keri G Mohror

LOSING CASSIE, FINDING PEACE
COPYRIGHT 2014 Kathy Matchinsky
Al rights reserved
Additional copies available by emailing cassiesbook24@gmail.com

Acknowledgements

First of all, I would like to thank my beautiful angel in heaven, Cassie, for giving me the reassurance that she is still here amongst us; I just can't see her. I feel her presence all around me. To my friends and family, thank you for sharing all the visits you had from her. All these things are what kept me strong. And my belief in Jesus Christ that she is by his side and as beautiful as she was on Earth; I will see her again someday, only the Lord knows that day. Just Believe! My hope is that this book gives other parents who have lost children hope. Have faith that there is so much more going on than we could ever imagine. My belief is, death is not the end.

The Lord is close to the brokenhearted and saves those who are crushed in spirit.

Jesus Christ our Lord and Savior

There's no tragedy in life like the death of a child. Things never get back to the way they were.

Dwight D. Eisenhower
American President

Table of Contents

Prologue

Chapter 1: An Ordinary Life

Chapter 2: The World Turned Upside Down

Chapter 3: Days of Hope and Heartbreak

Chapter 4: Signs in Silver

Chapter 5: A Sense of Presence

Chapter 6: Reassurances

Chapter 7: Letting Go, Moving On

Afterword: Cassie's Bridge

Prologue

There are moments, when you are walking through the darkness, that you believe, the sun will never shine again. And there are other moments, when the sun does appear, or a fresh, warm breeze caresses your face, or you drive by a playground filled with laughing children ... and you are suddenly angry. Because how could there, why *should* there be, light and joy and life still in the world.

Such is the nature of grief.

On this early fall morning, though, I welcome the sun. We are finally having the roof re-shingled — one of those mundane jobs that get pushed to the side while you're living every day in crisis mode. As I putter around the house, I hear the footsteps of the workmen above me, the scrape of metal tools against asphalt shingles, shouted instructions between the men as they work. It's all so normal. Normal feels good.

I'm a little surprised when the doorbell rings and I find our contractor, Kenny, standing on the step. We've known him for a long time, but the young man working with him today is a stranger. I smile at Ken. "Something I can do for you?"

"Tim found this on the roof." He holds out his hand, revealing a shiny dime.
I stare at the piece of silver, small and bright on his beefy, calloused palm. "Do you often find coins on rooftops?" I ask finally, glancing up into his honest, open expression.

He shakes his head and shrugs. "First time ever."

Kenny hands me the dime. "I thought I might as well give it to you; I'm guessing it must be yours." He gives me a friendly smile and turns to go back to his work.

I watch him go, then quietly close the door. The dime feels warm and solid in my fist. I close my eyes and my lips murmur almost soundlessly.

"Thank you, Cassie."

Chapter 1: An Ordinary Life

Most of my life has been completely normal — some might even say ordinary. Fine by me. My dreams and aspirations growing up were the same as most girls of my generation. Oh, I dreamed of an "exciting" career; in my case, as a stewardess flying around the world to places a lot more exotic than little Perham, Minnesota, where I grew up.

I was the youngest of seven: four boys and three girls. We lived on a farm until I was eight or nine, and some of my fondest memories are of going with my brothers to get the cows, playing hide-and-seek in the corn rows, riding the flexible limbs of willows and pretending they were my pony.

By the time I got to high school we had moved off the farm. I started volunteering at a local nursing home, and working there when I turned 16. The work was rewarding – my first taste of care giving. Little did I know how those experiences would prepare me for what was to come. No, not prepare; nothing can prepare you for certain kinds of pain. But it gave me a strong emotional foundation and skills that would be needed some day.

In the end, I didn't become a stewardess. I married Rick, my best friend's brother, and moved with him to the small, central Minnesota town of Alexandria, where Rick was going to school for marketing and sales. We settled down and had kids – first Shannon, in 1978, then Shane, two years later. Like I said, it was a normal life. Rick was busy with work, and was an avid fisherman and hunter, so

I was alone with the kids a lot. I suppose you could say I kind of raised them myself, but that was okay. It was the 1980s, and that's how things were then. I was a wife and a mom, and it was a good life.

By the time the kids were 10 and 12, Rick and I were starting to think in terms of "after." After the kids are grown and gone, we'll be able to travel, redecorate, relax … Then all those plans came crashing down one day in the summer of 1989 when I got some unexpected news.

I was pregnant.

—

I'd like to say I was thrilled to learn that our third child was on the way. But the truth is, I wasn't. In fact, I was devastated. We weren't equipped for a new baby — literally, since I'd long since given away all the old baby things — and even more so, emotionally. I was 34 years old, still five years younger than my own mom was when she had me, but still the mere thought of starting over again exhausted me. The diapers, the sleepless nights, the terrible twos … I couldn't face it.

And it wasn't supposed to have happened! We'd agreed there wouldn't be any more kids, and Rick had even been scheduled for a vasectomy. But the doctor got the flu and postponed the procedure for a week, and … well, here we were again. Expecting.
I suppose I should have taken that as a sign, but at the time I was in a blind panic. Looking back, it seems like I wasn't really in my right

mind, because I did something I would never in a million years have believed I would. I made an appointment to have an abortion.

We didn't tell Shannon and Shane what was going on, though they probably sensed the emotional turmoil Rick and I were going through. On the morning of my appointment, as Rick and I were getting ready to leave, nine-year-old Shane suddenly became very upset. He had no idea where we were going — but he did NOT want us to go. He was so inconsolable that I finally looked at Rick and said, "Maybe we're not meant to do this." So we canceled, and on March 6, 1990, Cassidy Ann Matchinsky was born.

Knowing what I do now, I wonder sometimes how our lives would have been different if I'd kept that appointment. God knows we would have been spared a mountain of pain and fear and grief. But we also wouldn't have had 14 years with Cassie. And in spite of everything, I wouldn't give that up for the world.

Chapter 2: A World Turned Upside Down

Cass was such a happy, beautiful little girl. We were so blessed!

Whatever our fears and misgivings while I was pregnant, we all were over the moon
about that little, pink bundle of joy when she arrived — our perfect, if unexpected,
gift from God. Of course there were adjustments, and those sleepless nights and dirty diapers were definitely part of the deal. But there were also first smiles, first words, first steps. So many

little moments that swell your heart with an intensity of joy and a powerful love that is different from anything else.

For her first eight years, Cassie was just a regular kid. She was smart and funny; we called her our little spitfire. She liked school and dreamed of being a writer when she grew up. She loved music: the Styxx song "Come Sail Away" was her absolute favorite. She was outgoing and had lots of friends. She enjoyed bowling, played basketball and baseball on a local Little League team. Like every child, she got her share of colds, the flu, the usual stomach aches. It was all so normal — the familiar milestones and day-to-day ups and downs of childhood.

Cassie and her best friend, Britt. Such happy days!

Then in the winter of 1998, Cassie came down with what we figured was the usual bout of flu that everybody seems to get that time of year. But this bug seemed more severe than usual, and hung on long after we would ordinarily expect her to bounce back. We took her to the doctor. And took her again. And again.

"It's a virus," they told us. "It has to run its course."

But Cassie was sicker than we'd ever seen her, and it seemed to get worse and worse. She had so much congestion, more mucus than I'd ever seen anybody produce. Finally, in desperation, I brought her in to the Emergency Room. More blood tests, and finally a diagnosis: mononucleosis, that common virus that is laughingly called the "kissing disease," because so many teenagers pass it along in their saliva. It's usually caused by the Epstein-Barr virus, and most often strikes teens and young adults. So at age eight, Cassie was a little young for it. They put our little girl in the hospital, gave her fluids and antibiotics and steroids. And finally she began to get better.

Every parent hates to see their child sick or hurting. But we figured it was just another one of those rites of passage, an unpleasant but temporary episode in the life of an otherwise happy, healthy child. "This too shall pass," as the saying goes. And it did.

Or at least we thought it did. Cassie went back to school. Maybe she was a little more tired than usual, or didn't have that little spark that was there before ... I honestly don't know. In the hustle and bustle of everyday life, perhaps little signs can be missed. But Cassie seemed well, and didn't complain. Everything seemed normal. We know now it wasn't.

We first noticed something was wrong that summer. Cassie was playing baseball in the summer rec program. She'd always been a decent athlete — no superstar, but she could hold her own with the other kids.

One afternoon, however, I noticed she was having trouble hitting the ball. Somehow she just couldn't coordinate her swing with the pitch. I watched her strike out again and again, and began to feel a vague uneasiness. It was just so unlike her. Coincidentally, our family doctor happened to be standing next to me, watching the game; his child was also on the team. I remember remarking to him on how strange it was that Cassie was struggling. But after the game Cassie seemed fine, and I let it go. Anybody can have an off day, right?

Not long after that, it all hit the fan. Cassie was sick again. Really sick. She was so tired, felt so ill. More doctor visits. More tests. More inconclusive results. One morning she stumbled out of her room. She looked so terrible, so sick. I was alarmed. "We're going back to the doctor," I said. She just shrugged miserably. "Why?" she answered. "They don't do anything anyway." She lay down on the couch while I went to her room to get some clothes.

When I came back, my daughter was moaning unintelligibly. Before my eyes, Cassie was slipping into a coma.
Much of that day, and many days after, is a blur. I remember Cassie on the couch, unresponsive. I remember calling 911. By a cruel coincidence, there had been two car accidents that morning, so the local ambulance service was tied up elsewhere. An off-duty paramedic on her way somewhere happened to hear the call on her pager. Knowing the situation, she turned her car around and drove to the emergency station. She took out an ambulance herself and

drove to our home, carried Cassie out of the house and drove her to the hospital. I followed the ambulance, driven by a neighbor.

At the hospital, I called the other kids at school. A nurse asked me, "Do you think you might want to contact your husband?" That's how out of it I was; it hadn't even occurred to me until that moment. But Rick was out of town that day, fishing with a friend near Detroit Lakes, about 80 miles away. That area has many lakes, and I knew the guys would want to try as many as they could. Unfortunately, I only recalled the name of one lake I knew they would be fishing.

Our Cassie had so many friends. It was hard seeing her so much alone after she got sick.

The nurse offered to contact the sheriff's office for me in the hopes they could locate him. Unbelievably, the sheriff ran into Rick and his friend just as they were packing up to leave that lake. Another few minutes, and there would have been no way to find him. I just can't believe that was a coincidence.

Rick raced back to Alexandria and we met with our daughter's pediatrician, Dr. Carlsen. Based on Cassie's symptoms, he told us, he suspected meningitis. "I think we can handle it here," he said, "but I'm not too proud to tell you, if you want her to take her to the Twin Cities, you go."

My husband and I looked at each other, and knew immediately what we had to do. "Let's go."

Chapter 3: Days of Hope and Heartbreak

They flew Cassie to Children's Hospital in Minneapolis immediately, and thank God they did. If she hadn't been transferred, Cassie would have died that day. Our small hospital simply wasn't equipped to deal with what was going on with our daughter.

Meanwhile, Rick and I were making the nerve-wracking drive to the Twin Cities, two hours away. It happened to be during the Minneapolis Aquatennial, the biggest summer festival in the city, so traffic was a nightmare. At one point a medical helicopter flew over us, going the other way, back toward Alexandria. Of course I feared the worst. We didn't know until we reached the hospital that it wasn't her.

No one who hasn't experienced it can understand how frightening and disorienting it is to walk into a hospital, not knowing if your child is alive or dead, being surrounded by what seems like every doctor in the place, and they're all firing questions at you. To go from a perfectly normal day to having your whole world turned upside down. It was like a dream ... except you don't wake up. Cassie was intubated when we got there, and still unconscious. They were running all kinds of tests, and finally someone told us, "We think we know what this is. Let's try steroids." That was Saturday night. By Sunday night she had begun to come around, and on Monday morning she was extubated and talking to us.

Her doctor gave us the diagnosis: Acute, disseminated encephalomyelitis, or ADEM. It's a rare auto-immune disorder, occurring in only eight people per million, mostly kids between five and eight, and usually follows a viral infection. ADEM creates lesions on the brain and spinal cord similar to those seen in multiple sclerosis, and the disease is sometimes mistaken for that disorder. It's treated with steroids. The good news, we learned, is that 90% of patients recover either fully or with only minor after effects.

As her world got smaller, Cassie's beloved dog Abby became her closest companion

Cassie was in the hospital for six days, and then we took her home, thanking our lucky stars that we'd come through that nightmare and had our girl back. But our relief wouldn't last. Cassie remained on steroids to control the inflammation in her brain, and whenever they tried to wean her off them, the infection flared up again. She was diagnosed with MDEM: Multiphasic disseminated encephalomyelitis, the chronic form of ADEM.

And thus began a five-year merry-go-round of hospital visits, medications, periods of hope, moments of despair. While Cassie was on steroids, the inflammation and scary symptoms were kept at bay. But the steroids came with their own horrors: kidney damage, bone weakness, increased susceptibility to infection and, most cruelly for a little girl on the cusp of adolescence, development of "moon face," caused by shifting of body fat to the face. Off the steroids, the lesions grew and Cassie experienced vision problems, difficulty with balance. It was a lose-lose situation.

A year after her initial diagnosis there was another devastating setback. Cassie was diagnosed with a second auto-immune disease: Chronic Inflammatory Demyelinating Polyradiculoneuropathy (CIPD). Now, in addition to her brain and spinal cord, her peripheral nervous system was under attack. This brought numbness, tingling in the limbs, and progressive muscle weakness. There were times she was so weak that she couldn't even hold a pencil. Walking became difficult, and eventually she was confined to a wheelchair. We tried every kind of therapy offered to us, grabbed at every scrap of hope. She underwent plasma immunoglobulin replacement therapy, an experimental procedure at the time. Antibodies from healthy donors were introduced into her bloodstream in an attempt to recalibrate her faulty immune system. As far as we could tell, it had no effect.

Cassie continued to get worse. We tried to give our daughter as normal a life as possible. Over the next several years, she attended school when she was up to it, and had a tutor when she was too weak to go. As time went by, Cassie's world became smaller and smaller. Her friends dropped away. I don't blame them — Cassie wasn't able to play with them like she used to, she looked different and was so disabled. Kids don't know how to handle something like that. But I know it hurt Cassie. She was a little girl, facing something no child should have to, living in an adult world before she was even a teen.

The final blow came when Cassie developed a third autoimmune disorder, autoimmune hemolytic anemia. Basically, her body was attacking her own blood, destroying blood cells faster than she could make them. She would swell up with fluid. Peripheral nerve damage made movement so excruciating that she couldn't even roll over in bed by herself. We brought her into our bed so we could turn her and make her more comfortable.

Her doctors told us they'd never heard of a case where one person contracted three such devastating autoimmune disorders. Most people, who get one of these diseases, for whatever reason, recover and have normal lives. Our Cassie was different. They suspect she must have had some "chink" in her DNA that allowed that original virus to take hold, then, turn her own body's defenses against her. Perhaps if she had been treated earlier, when she first came down with mono, when this infection first started to fester in her brain, things might have been different ... but who knows?

As a last resort, her doctors put Cassie on Cyclosporin, a potent immunosuppressant generally prescribed after organ transplants. It helped for a while, but we knew it couldn't be a long-term solution. It's simply too toxic to the body. In any case, its beneficial effect was only temporary.

Cassie's final weeks were spent in Children's Hospital, trying to stave off the inevitable. She coded several times, only to be brought back to us by modern medical technology. It gave us a little more time.

Only a little.

Cassie had a blanket she'd kept since she was a baby. Over the years it had become pretty ratty, but it gave her comfort. It was something familiar, a reminder of her life before. One morning they took Cassie for still more tests, and while she was out of her room her bed linens were removed for laundering. As far as we can tell, her blanket must have been tangled up in the sheets. We never saw it again. Did I consider it an omen at the time? I don't remember. But it wasn't long after that when things got really bad.

Her condition was increasingly unstable. Once they intubated Cassie for a test, and she crashed. Rick and I were hustled into a tiny waiting room while a defibrillator shocked my little girl again and again. They brought her back that time. She regained consciousness and we were able to talk with her, comfort her as best we could.

The hospital has a laundry room for use by families of long-term patients. I was doing a load one morning while Cassie was having a CT scan. As I tossed our few articles of clothing into a dryer, our minister appeared in the doorway. I knew what that meant. While undergoing the scan ... something happened. Cassie never regained consciousness, and seven days later she died.
It was May 7, 2004 — two days before Mother's Day. Cassie was 14 years old.

Four days later we laid our youngest child to rest. As I stood beside her grave, silently saying my final goodbye, it seemed my journey with Cassie had come to an end. In reality, it was just beginning.

Chapter 4: Signs in Silver

For most of my life, the concept of an afterlife wasn't something I gave a lot of thought to. Raised a Christian, I just accepted what I'd been taught from childhood: that if you are a good person, you go to heaven after you die; if you are bad, you go the other place. Caught up in the business of day-to-day living, I didn't worry much about where I was going — I figured I'd find out when I got there.

When you lose someone close to you, especially a child, your perspective changes. Suddenly it becomes very important to know that there is something more than this world, that you will see your loved one again. But can we ever really know? Conventional religion tells us we must rely on faith. Yet faith feels like cold comfort when you've been praying your heart out for five years and your little girl dies anyway.

Don't get me wrong. I never blamed God for Cassie's illness. He knows all of our time on earth: when it starts and when it ends. But the answer I got to my prayers wasn't the one I wanted. My child was gone, and I was wracked with grief and fear. Was she all right, wherever she was? Was she happy? Did she know how much she was loved, how deeply she was missed by those she left behind?

Despite my anguish and uncertainty, the possibility that my daughter could reach across the divide between us never occurred to me. Ghost stories were for Halloween, and angels were pretty ladies with halos and gossamer wings that perched on top of the Christmas tree.

Then, not long after Cassie passed, Rick and I were visiting with Rick's Uncle Jim and Aunt Rose at their home. I was sitting alone on their couch, my back to a large picture window. We were simply chatting, when suddenly a bird crashed into the window behind me, then flew away. Strangely, the bird had left an impression on the window that looked remarkably like a winged figure: an angel. It seemed an odd occurrence, but after remarking on it, we shrugged it off and continued talking. Then ... THUD. Another bird hit the window, this time on the other side of me. This one, too, left the same familiar silhouette. My friends said it looked like I had a pair of angels on my shoulders. Now, I've witnessed a lot of birds crash into windows in my lifetime, but I've never seen one leave that kind of impression — let alone two. As crazy as it seemed, I couldn't help wondering if the incident was more than a coincidence.

Rose mentioned in passing that she had another friend who had lost a child, and since his death his parents had been finding dimes in random places. I couldn't imagine what dimes had to do with the loss of a loved one, so I didn't think much about it. But I'd soon have reason to remember that conversation.

My desperation to know about Cassie led me to the local library, where I started reading about life after life, paranormal activity, anything I could find that might help me understand where my daughter was now, or at least find some comfort for our terrible loss. I've always been a practical person, and to be honest, a lot of what I was reading seemed pretty far-fetched. Still, it seemed like a lot of people in this world have had experiences they can't explain. I didn't really expect to be one of them.

Then the dimes started appearing.

We'd find them in the oddest places. For me, it was most often in the washing machine. Never a quarter or a nickel or a penny, mind you. Only dimes. I always check the pockets of clothes before I put them in the machine, so I know they weren't coming from there. Rick found dimes in his truck, in parking lots, on docks where he fished. Soon we began hearing from friends and relatives that they were finding dimes, too. They showed up in people's shoes, on window ledges, between the sheets of freshly made beds. One morning my brother-in-law got out of bed and his wife noticed he had a dime stuck to his bare back! "I'd just changed the bedding," my sister-in-law told me, "and I KNOW there was no money in that bed when I made it!"

Cassie and her daddy shared a special bond

I've since discovered that, finding dimes is very common when someone has passed over. In fact, a Google search using the words "spirit" and "dimes" yields more than 1.3 MILLION results. There seem to be lots of theories about why spirits would choose coins, and especially dimes, as a sign for their loved ones. It may be that coins are something we're likely to notice when they show up in an unexpected place, as opposed to some other random object that we might just ignore. As the saying goes, "Money talks!" Interestingly, it appears that pennies used to be the coinage of choice for spirit messages, but have been replaced in recent decades by dimes. I guess they even have inflation in heaven!

The dimes just kept coming. Often they were found in places where dimes just plain shouldn't be! For instance, one of Rick's hunting buddies was way up north bear hunting in a remote part of the state. The only sign of civilization for miles was a ramshackle, mice-infested shack that hadn't seen human occupation for years. The hunting party set up camp in the old structure. On the third morning, Rick's friend had just crawled out of his sleeping bag and was putting on his shoes when he found a dime lying on the floor.

Cassie's sense of humor seems to shine through in some of these instances. On that same hunting trip, the guys toted their "porta-potty" way out into the brush for privacy. One afternoon one of the hunters was … ahem … "meditating" on the privy, when his glance was caught by something shining in the tall weeds nearby. You guessed it: Cassie had paid a call!

Rick seems to find dimes most often while he's hunting or fishing, two activities that help him feel at peace. While staying in his Dad's hunting lodge – a bunkhouse with a loft containing a dozen or more bunks – Rick found a dime next to the very bed he'd chosen to sleep in. I can still see the grin on Rick's face when he reached into his pocket and pulled out that dime to show me. Another time, Rick and several friends found dimes in and under their sleeping bags in the deer shack.

As Cassie became sicker, the love and support of her sister and brother were so important

Cassie seems to enjoy tweaking people who don't believe these experiences are real. One day, friends were over with their young son. We told them about the mysterious dimes we'd been finding. The son was what you might call a "Doubting Thomas." Truth be told, he thought we were full of baloney! The visit came to an end and we said goodbye to them and watched as their car pulled away. Suddenly it stopped. The back door opened and the young boy bounded out, grinning from ear to ear. He ran up to us, shouting, "Look what I just found on the back seat!"

I think you know the rest of the story!

A lot of the dimes have been found in places that aren't so out of the ordinary: on a coffee table, lying on the floor, on a chair at a restaurant, at the bottom of an otherwise empty purse. By themselves, these might seem like nothing special. But in many cases, they have been found in places where the finder KNEW there had not been a coin only a moment before. A friend told me of one day at the office when a colleague was working on a chart. The women took a quick coffee break, and when they returned there was a single dime on top of the chart on her desk. This co-worker didn't know anything about Cassie or the dimes ... but my friend knew that that dime appeared there for a reason.
Another time I was chatting on the phone with a close friend. I happened to tell her about the dimes we were finding, and a couple of minutes later I heard her gasp. "Oh, my God!" she said. "I was sweeping the kitchen while we were talking, and I just found a dime on the floor!"

One of the most unusual places I've found a dime was at a local "big box" home improvement store. I'd stopped in to pick up a particular kind of screw I needed for a project. The screw section consisted of dozens of little drawers, each containing plastic packets of different sized screws. I opened a drawer, pulled out a packet – and there, tucked in with the screws in the package, was a dime. It wasn't the size screw I was looking for, but you can bet I bought that packet anyway!

I will always be grateful for one particular sign. A few months after Cassie died, her brother Shane was married. I wanted so badly for

Cassie to be there celebrating with us. At the groom's dinner, we found a dime between two tables. The next night, after the wedding and reception, our friend Sandy and her husband returned to their hotel room to find a dime in the center of the bed. Do I think Cassie was present for her brother's big day? Oh, yes. Cassie even found a chance to tease her bro a few months after the wedding. Shane had been feeling a little slighted because he hadn't found any dimes. One day, he was doing a little cleaning around the house. When he finished, he sat down on the couch to watch TV. And right there on the coffee table, where he had previously cleaned, lay a shiny new dime.

More than anything, I think it's the sheer volume of dimes found by so many of the people who knew and loved Cassie that makes me believe these occurrences are more than mere coincidence. Sure, everybody finds a coin once in a while — in my fifty-odd years I've stooped to pick up a few random quarters and pennies and nickels. But never in my life have I experienced such a concentration of unusual findings. So many dimes, and *only* dimes. In that first year, Rick and I alone found 32 dimes.

Even so, I could almost convince myself that these things were just the result of the over-active imagination of a grieving mom who wants desperately to know her child is all right.
But dimes aren't the only signs we've had from our Cassie.

Chapter 5: A Sense of Presence

It seems television is crowded these days with reality shows about the paranormal. There's "Ghost Hunters," "Hauntings," "Paranormal Witness," even "Celebrity Ghost Stories." Obviously there are a lot of people out there who have experienced things they can't explain — whether it's mysterious sounds, objects moving or even just a feeling that someone is watching over you. Some people scoff at these accounts, but having experienced a lot of them myself, I believe.

Cassie was crazy about her nephew Brady. She would have been such a wonderful mom.

I've felt Cassie's presence many times, and so have many others. Shannon regularly has the feeling that her baby sister is nearby, riding in the car with her or looking over her shoulder at work. I've felt her beside me as I stood at the stove. Strangely, it's children, most of whom never even knew Cassie, who seem most attuned to her presence. When my niece's son was small, he often spoke of and to Cassie.

All of my four granddaughters, all born after Cassie passed, have encountered her. They started making odd comments at about age 2. Once I observed one of the little girls staring intently at something I couldn't see. "What are you looking at?" I asked her, puzzled. "There's Cassie," she answered, still gazing at the doorway. "She's coming down the stairs right now."

My granddaughter Maggie also has a connection to the auntie she never met. One summer evening, Maggie was outside on the patio with her mom Shannon and her mom's friend. Maggie kept pointing at the neighbor's roof and saying, "Look, mommy!" Since she was busy talking with her friend, Shannon didn't pay much attention. But after 10 minutes of this, Shannon finally got frustrated. "What are you looking at?" she asked her daughter. "It's Cassie, mommy," she answered matter-of-factly. "She's holding a puppy."

We found this in a jacket pocket after Cassie died – no idea where it came from

Last summer the family gathered at our house to celebrate Rick and my anniversary. We were all enjoying the festivities in the backyard when Olivia, my step-granddaughter, came to me. "Cassie is here," she said. I felt a little shiver go down my spine. "She is?" I said. Olivia nodded and pointed to one corner of the yard. "She's over there." I told her to tell Cassie thanks for coming to celebrate with us. Olivia calmly walked to that place in the yard and seemed to have a brief conversation with someone. I truly believe our youngest child came to be with us on that special occasion.

There have been other weird occurrences over the years since Cassie passed. Rick and I have heard noises coming from Cassie's bedroom, and one time after hearing rummaging sounds I discovered her little jewelry box standing open, its contents in disarray as if someone had been searching for something in it.

Some time after Cassie's death, I finally found the strength to sort through her clothes. Curiously, I found a stone in a pocket of one of her wind breakers; it was embossed with a fossil imprint of a dragonfly. Neither Rick nor I have any idea where she might have gotten this pretty little ornament; we didn't give it to her, and can't think of a time when someone else might have. Later I learned a little about the spiritual significance of dragonflies in many cultures. It is often seen as a symbol of transformation. In Japanese lore, the dragonfly represents joy and new light, and serve as guides for souls when they revisit their loved ones on earth.

I like that idea.

Electronics seem to be a vehicle for Cassie's sense of humor. Our television has a habit of turning itself off and on; the same thing happens with computers and radios. On one occasion Rick and I were away from home for the day. When we got home that evening, we heard a buzzing sound coming from the garage. We discovered that the switch for the live well in Rick's boat was flipped on. Rick hadn't used the boat in more than a week, and the live well battery has a short life; it would have been dead if it had been left on for any length of time. Cassie knew how much her Dad loves fishing – I think this was her way of telling us she remembers that.

Our good friend was close to Cassie during her lifetime. One night after she passed he awoke with a start, feeling certain that there was someone in the room with him. He was scared to death! He even called out, "All right, whoever is there, come and get me!" After some time he fell asleep again ... only to be jarred out of bed by the sound of his stereo blasting at full volume. Did I mention he lives alone?

Another time he was driving with his sons in the back seat when suddenly one of the boys' windows rolled down. He swore he wasn't touching it, and neither was their dad. There was another incident with the truck where the power locks started going up and down by themselves.

I was making dinner one night, feeling low and thinking about Cassie, when suddenly the fan on the microwave started, blowing on the highest setting. I couldn't shut it off until I tripped the circuit breaker. It hasn't happened again, and the microwave has worked perfectly ever since.

It seems Cassie has even tried to reach us through telecommunications technology. Not too long after we lost Cassie, Rick's mom phoned us in a panic. She said Rick's Uncle Jim's cell phone showed he'd received two calls from Douglas County Hospital, the medical facility here in Alexandria where Cassie had been treated so many times. No message was left. Jim has never had any contact with the hospital and isn't local. Could it really be a coincidence that someone at this small hospital in another part of the country would somehow misdial a long-distance call to a member of Cassie's family? We never found out who placed those calls, or what they wanted.

How about this: A while back we gave up our land line and switched entirely to cell phone service. One night at supper time, the phone on the wall rang.

The phone that supposedly had no service.

I picked up the receiver and heard only static and distant, unintelligible voices on the other end. "It must just be a fluke," Rick said. "If it's still connected, there can still be random activity on the line." I removed the cover of the phone and showed Rick the cord.

Unplugged.

Cassie seems to know when we need her most. The first Christmas Eve after she died, Rick and I were alone at home. We were both feeling pretty low. Trying to improve our mood, we decided to put on some holiday music. As we shuffled through the stacks of music CDs, we came across one we hadn't seen before. It was labeled "Cassie's CD," and it contained songs about angels. When had Cassie made it? We'll never know. But we do know that somehow our daughter felt our deep sorrow that special evening, and sent us comfort.

Cassie loved music. Often when Rick and I are driving someplace, talking about Cassie, her favorite song will come on the radio. For some reason, she was crazy about the song "Come Sail Away," by Styx. It came out in 1977 and isn't exactly in heavy rotation on most stations. The lyrics are haunting:

"I'm sailing away, set an open course for the virgin sea

'Cause I've got to be free ...

A gathering of angels appeared above my head.

They sang to me this song of hope and this is what they said:

They said come sail away, come sail away, come sail away with me ..."

Chapter 6: Reassurances

Then there are the dreams. We've all had them: Rick and I, Cassie's sister and brother, our friends and neighbors. Sometimes she's with us, doing some mundane thing like riding in a car — the kind of thing she would be doing if she were still with us. In these dreams, Cassie is healthy and happy. She looks so pretty, like she did before the steroids bloated her face. That was one of the hardest things for her. I remember her crying, telling me, "I'm so ugly." Of course she was always beautiful in my eyes, but it makes me happy to think that in heaven she looks the way she wanted to look, the way she felt most like herself.

My favorite dream was one where Cassie and I were at the hospital with one of her doctors. She was talking with the doctor in such a mature, confident way. I remember her saying to him, "What's the big deal?" I think that was her way of letting me know that she's okay now — that all the pain and sorrow of this world

Cass loved to snuggle with me and her nephew Brady

ultimately doesn't matter when we've moved on to a better place.

I can't help feeling a little envious of a powerful experience Rick had a couple of years after Cassie passed. He and his Dad had gone to Shannon's place in Phoenix on a fishing trip. Rick slept on an inflatable mattress in the loft. About 5:00 am, he was suddenly wide awake, feeling like someone was watching him. That wasn't so unusual; as I've mentioned, we often sense Cassie's presence near us. This time was different. Suddenly he felt a weight on his legs, as if someone were crawling over him. There was a sensation of someone lying next to him, and when he turned to look, there was Cassie. She was tucked in under the covers, cuddled up to him just like she did when she was little.

As her world got smaller, Cassie's beloved dog Abby became her closest companion

Rick remembers telling Cassie he loved her and holding her hand, which felt warm. They talked for a little while, though Rick doesn't remember exactly what they said. Finally Cassie told him she had to go. He felt her crawl back across his chest and get off the bed, and he watched her walk away. He held her hand as long as he could, but finally she slipped away. She looked back at him once, smiling, and then disappeared.

Rick said Cassie looked healthy and beautiful. And she was WALKING, something she hadn't been able to do for a long time before she died. Both Rick and I cried when he shared this experience with me. Was it a dream? Rick swears he wasn't sleeping, that he *knows* Cassie was really there with him that early morning. I guess it doesn't really matter. We both believe Cassie wanted us to know that she's still with us, and she's all right.

I wish I could say I've had that kind of close encounter with Cassie. There have been times when she has felt so close that I felt if only I turned around fast enough, I'd see her standing there. I have seen unexpected shadows out of the corner of my eye. Others have, too.

Our neighbor was over one evening. We were sitting around in the kitchen center island chatting when suddenly he got a strange look on his face. "Is there someone else here?" he asked. When we told him no, he went a little pale. "I just saw someone walk through the living room," he said. The figure was shadowy, but distinct.

Near Christmas another friend who has had several experiences of Cassie, joined our family at my son Shane's home for the holiday. We were talking when suddenly he asked, "Is the dog outside?" I told him it was. "Well, I just saw a shadow go down the hallway," he said.
I'm glad that Cassie was there to spend Christmas with us.

My friend Cathy had a phone consultation with a noted psychic. During the course of the conversation, Cathy mentioned she had a friend who had lost a daughter. "I know," the psychic said. "She visits often, usually around 3:00 am, and she leaves coins. They will know when she's present because they will notice an unusual smell."

When Cathy told me this, I was stunned. In fact, I often walk into a room and detect a chemical smell, like the solution used in beauty parlors to give permanents. Others have smelled it, too. I have no idea why Cassie would pick that pungent scent to announce her presence, but I've smelled it so many different times, in different places, that I have to believe the psychic knew what she was talking about.

Chapter 7: Letting Go, Moving On

Our language has expressions to describe the effect of great sorrow on the body. We say we are heartsick. Heavy-hearted. Our heart is broken. You learn how apt those metaphors are when you live with the weight of grief. Despite all the ways Cassie communicated that she was all right, I still missed my little girl so terribly. There were so many sleepless night, so many times some small thing could remind me of her and suddenly the pain was as sharp and fresh as it was the day she died.

That first Mother's Day, almost exactly a year after Cassie passed, was especially hard for me. It seemed like the signs that had been so frequent and clear in the first few months were becoming less often now. Cassie felt further away, and I wanted so desperately to hold her close to me.
That day I went out to the cemetery and cried my heart out. I talked to Cassie. I told her how much I missed her and how I felt she was forgetting about us, wherever she was now. It felt good to let it all out. I stayed there a long time, alone, in the peaceful place where our daughter was resting.

The next day I was visited a local store that was selling fresh, spring flowers. I selected a few for my garden, and as I turned to put them in my cart, my eye was caught by something on the dirt under my feet. It was a dime. Later, while sitting in the car, I went to take a pill. It slipped from my fingers and fell between the seats. I fished around under the seat for it. I didn't find the pill ... but my fingers closed around something cool and flat and familiar. It was a dime. And then, soon after, I went to my job at a home improvement store early in the morning. The parking lot was mostly empty at 5:00 am, and the street lights were still lit in the predawn darkness. As I headed from my car toward the store, I suddenly glimpsed something shining like a diamond on the cold, dark pavement. A dime: the third unexpected discovery in less than a week. I knew that Cassie had heard my anguish on Mother's Day and wanted me to know she was still with us. Still, there was an emptiness inside me.

Knowing how I was struggling, a friend recommended that I try Reiki. It's an Oriental spiritual practice that promotes physical and spiritual healing through the placement of the practitioner's hands on and over the body. We have a practitioner in Alexandria, who is much in demand. One day there happened to be an opening and I grabbed it. When I arrived for my appointment, Michelle (the practitioner) said, "I knew you were coming, because Cassie is here." Michelle told me that Cassie had given her guidance on how to treat me during our session.

I lay down on the table and Michelle began to move her hands over me. She told me that Cassie wanted her to concentrate on my heart – the heaviness there that was dragging me down. She worked a long time to dislodge this spiritual weight from inside me. As Michelle worked she spoke to me quietly about what she was feeling. She was sensing flowers and a casket. After the treatment, Michelle and I talked about what it all meant. We figured out that the heaviness represented Cassie's vault and casket, and the flowers were a symbol of her funeral. Michelle said Cassie wanted me to understand that I should not hold on to those things in my heart, because that's not where she was. Cassie wanted my soul to be as free of sorrow and pain as she is now.

We keep this memorial stone on the deck – I look at it often, and remember …

Something changed for me that day. I still miss Cassie, but I've come to a place of acceptance. My daughter is never far from my thoughts, but I try to focus on the happy memories and my gratitude that she is safe and happy and well – and that we were gifted with these many signs to comfort us.

Still, the memories – good and painful – remain. Not long ago, as my own mother lay dying, I was taken back to those terrible days of Cassie's illness. Not long before she died, we "celebrated" Easter while Cassie was in the hospital. It wasn't much of a holiday, as Cassie wasn't doing well. I was alone with her in her room that morning. She was very calm – then suddenly she began speaking, but I couldn't understand her. It sounded like a foreign language. I caught a few familiar words: "Jesus" and "path." After a moment, she looked up at me and asked, "Am I dead?" I assured her she wasn't, that she couldn't be talking to me if she were. She just shrugged, as if whatever it was she had seen or heard was the most normal thing in the world – nothing to be afraid of.

Nearly a decade later, while at my mom's bedside, I experienced again one of those moments of other-worldliness, of profound holiness, that seems to accompany people whose earthly journey is nearing its close.

Like Cassie, Mom seemed to have access to some place that's off limits to the rest of us, almost as if, as we near death, we have one foot in this world and the other in the next. Like Cassie, mom started speaking to presences we couldn't see. She talked to my Dad, gone for many years. She conversed with Jesus. And, she told me in one of her last lucid moments, she saw Cassie. "Can you see heaven, Mom?" I asked her. "Yes," she answered softly. "It's beautiful. So many flowers."

Mom passed not long after that. I believe she and Dad and Cassie and so many other loved ones are together now, in a place where there are so many flowers.

Cassie has been gone almost 10 years now. If she were still with us, our little girl would be a young woman. I often wonder what she would be like. Would she have gone to college? Would she have a boyfriend, or a husband? Children of her own? Sometimes I look at her picture and try to imagine what she would look like, this beautiful, special child of mine. I think she would be tall and graceful and full of life. That is the image — the dream — I carry in my heart now.

I wouldn't wish this journey on anyone, yet I wouldn't trade the experience for the world. It has made me a more spiritual person, stronger, and more compassionate. Most of all, it has given me certainty that this world we inhabit for such a short time is not all there is. I know that Cassie is still with me, and I know I will see her again someday.

The signs come less often now; I think it's because when your loss is new, your loved ones know how desperately you need to know they are all right. But they also know that we here on earth need to move forward, to keep living. And so as our pain lessens over time, they are able to distance themselves.

Last year, Rick and I escaped to Arizona during the cold Minnesota winter. While there, we met a man who had a convertible he was trying to sell. It made me smile to see that car – it had always been a dream of mine and Cassie's to have a convertible, to feel the wind in our hair, the sun on our faces. It never happened while Cassie was alive ... maybe, I thought, that dream could be fulfilled in her memory. But it wasn't to be. We couldn't figure a way to get the car from one end of the country to the other. And so, regretfully, I let that dream go.

Then, this spring, we received a phone call from that same man. He was still trying to sell the convertible. If he found someone to drive it up to Minnesota, would we still be interested?
And so, on a bright spring day, Cassie's dream car arrived at our front door. It was exactly 10 years to the day since she had passed. Coincidence?

I don't think so.

We continue to be surprised by reminders that Cassie keeps watch over us. One day I was looking at her photo, and couldn't help saying out loud, "I miss you, Cassie. I wish you would visit me like you used to." After a while I went out to the mailbox. As I pulled the mail out, I heard a clinking sound. There, in the box, was a single dime.

Thank you, Cassie, for not forgetting about us. You and God know that we will never, ever forget you.

Afterword

At Cassie's funeral, a close family friend, Cathy Weber-Zunker, wrote and read this touching tribute. It says so much about who Cassie was, and how she continues to make a difference in so many lives.

Though only 14 years old, Cassie Ann Matchinsky has lived two separate lives. First, the life of a bouncy, innocent child. Here… she touched the hearts of kids and teachers with their playful character, delightful smile and witty sense of humor. Her blond shiny hair, brilliant smile and proud posture are the trademark of her elementary photos.

Then Cassie crossed over a bridge into an illness… a bridge to an adult world.

Without realizing it: she became a teacher for all of the grown-ups sitting here today. She has made us see and learn lessons that great scholars and teachers are unable to impart. Her lesson plan included teaching us kindness, tender-heartedness, compassion, and patience. She taught us to enjoy the HERE and the NOW.

Without realizing it: Cassie created a bridge for all of us to come together... she created a new family. Look around you here today - see the people you now know - the ones you have bonded with because Cassie brought all of us together.

Without realizing it: Cassie's demeanor forced medical staff to cross over a bridge - the bridge between head knowledge and human heart caring. She sucked them into the precious world of Cassie's family. She reached across the bridge and tugged on their heart strings. Her innocence beckoned them to her bedside day and night ... their own tears trying to wash away the sickness.

Without realizing it: Cassie, like the Pied Piper, has let us all across a bridge. It is to a new land that has taught us courage... Strength... Hope... and Determination. She has taught us to laugh in spite of pain. Never again will we be able to look at our lives in the same manner. She has raised the bar so high, that none of us who knew her will ever have just cause to feel sorry for ourselves.

Without realizing it: Cassie's illness taught all of US about life.

In 14 years, Cassie has created a legacy the rest of us will strive toward our entire lives with no hope of accomplishing.

We know very well, when it is our time to cross over; it will be Cassie's hand that will once again be reaching out. What will she say? She will say, "I've shown you how to cross over bridges my whole life. Here, take my hand, I will help you to cross one more time."

Made in the USA
Lexington, KY
19 November 2018